DISCOVER OUR
SOLAR SYSTEM

DISCOVER OUR
SOLAR SYSTEM

COLIN STUART

Illustrated by Charlie Brandon-King

Button
Books

CONTENTS

INTRODUCTION

Our busy lives make it easy to forget that we are just one small part in a huge solar system of planets, moons, dwarf planets, asteroids, and comets all swirling around the Sun. This amazing set of worlds is just one among billions of others in our galaxy, which in turn is just one of trillions in the universe. Staring up into the sky can really change the way you see the world.

We are so lucky to live at a time when we have the ability to understand how we fit into the whole cosmos in this way. Thousands of years ago people could only look at space with their eyes. Now we not only have telescopes, but can also send machines to explore the planets.

If you're reading this book to learn about the solar system for the first time, the future that lies ahead of you is so exciting. Chances are you'll see the first people walk on the surface of another planet. Human missions to Mars are already being planned. Soon the human race will leave their home planet for good and live and work elsewhere in the solar system. This book will show you all the amazing places there are to explore.

"Soon the human race will leave their home planet for good and live and work elsewhere in the solar system."

7

HOW IT ALL STARTED
THE BIG BANG

OUR UNIVERSE HASN'T BEEN AROUND FOREVER

Both space and time started in a cataclysmic event 13.8 billion years ago that astronomers call **The Big Bang**.

To begin with, the new universe was filled only with energy, but over time some of that energy was turned into atoms.

For the first 380,000 years, there was so much stuff flying around inside the new universe that light couldn't escape. Whenever it tried, it bumped into something and was knocked off course. Eventually the universe cooled enough and the light was let out all at once—astronomers call it the **Cosmic Microwave Background**.

TIME BEGINS

0.32 SECONDS

1.8 TRILLION°F

1 SECOND

100 SECONDS

1 YEAR

100 YEARS

STARTS TO COOL

380,000 YEARS

THE FIRST STARS

200 MILLION YEARS

1 BILLION YEARS

FIRST STARS AND GALAXIES

After a few hundred million years, gravity drew some of the universe's atoms together to make the first stars. Those stars gathered together into groups called galaxies. Astronomers estimate there are now two trillion galaxies in the universe, including ours—a beautiful spiral galaxy called **The Milky Way**.

OUR SOLAR SYSTEM

A gas cloud within the Milky Way collapsed around 4.6 billion years ago, setting off a chain of events that ignited the Sun. However, not all the atoms in that cloud made it into the Sun. Some were left in a flat disk around it that gravity slowly turned into the planets.

There are stars so far away that their light hasn't reached Earth.

Astronomers think an invisible "glue" called **dark matter** holds galaxies together. **Dark energy** is making the expansion of the universe speed up.

OUR SOLAR SYSTEM

THE MILKY WAY

The Milky Way belongs to a group of galaxies called **The Local Group**.

You are made of stardust!

The Sun wasn't the first star those atoms had been part of. An earlier star had exploded and blasted its atoms across the galaxy. Some of those atoms are now in the Sun, some are in the Earth, and some are in you.

10 BILLION YEARS

GALAXY CLUSTERS

Not all galaxies are spirals—ellipticals are shaped like footballs and lenticulars like cigars.

The observable universe is thought to be 93 billion light-years in diameter—and still expanding!

ICE LINE

THE SUN (page 14)

VENUS (page 18)

MERCURY (page 16)

MARS (page 24)

EARTH (page 20)

A group of asteroids known as the Trojans share Jupiter's orbit.

Astronomers have found nearly a million asteroids in the **Asteroid Belt** (page 36). A fifth rocky planet would have formed out of the material in the Asteroid Belt were it not for the gravity of Jupiter. The giant planet prevents these chunks of rock and metal left over from the formation of the solar system from sticking together.

JUPITER (page 26)

The giant planets probably didn't start out where they are today. Astronomers think that Jupiter has moved inward and the other three giant planets headed further from the Sun. It is even possible that Uranus and Neptune swapped order. We're lucky Jupiter stopped, otherwise it might have knocked into the Earth.

URANUS (page 30)

The planets' orbits are not circles. They are oval-shaped "ellipses."

SUN	MERCURY	VENUS	EARTH	MARS		JUPITER		SATURN
	0.4 AU	0.7 AU	1 AU	1.5 AU		5.2 AU		9.6 AU

OUR SOLAR SYSTEM

SATURN (page 28)

Temperatures in the early solar system were so high close to the Sun that everything but rock and metal was boiled away. That's why the inner four planets—Mercury, Venus, Earth, and Mars—are all small and solid. Earth's water and atmosphere were added later through volcanic eruptions and asteroid impacts from space.

Beyond a place called the "**ice line**," temperatures were a lot cooler. Some liquids and gases froze solid and gas gathered around them to make the giant planets. Jupiter and Saturn are "**gas giants**." Uranus and Neptune are "**ice giants**." Together, this large quartet are over 200 times heavier than the rocky planets.

The **Kuiper Belt** is a band of small objects orbiting the Sun beyond Neptune.

NEPTUNE (page 32)

Astronomers are starting to believe that there's a ninth planet in the solar system. They have seen small objects journeying around the Sun farther out than the **Kuiper Belt**. Their orbits are all lined up, suggesting something is herding them into these positions.
This "Planet Nine" would be bigger than Earth.

URANUS

As you can see here, the planets are not equally spaced out.

NEPTUNE

AU—ASTRONOMICAL UNIT (1 AU = 93 MILLION MILES)

19 AU

30 AU

DISCOVERING OUR SOLAR SYSTEM

Ancient people connected the stars to draw patterns called **constellations**.

GEOCENTRIC SOLAR SYSTEM

EARTH

Our early ancestors believed the Sun, Moon, and the planets all moved around the Earth. This made sense because it doesn't feel like the Earth is moving.

Astronomers call this a "**geocentric**" model, meaning **a central Earth**. It's an idea that remained popular for more than a thousand years.

Everything changed when we invented the **telescope** in the **1600s**—a device that allows us to see farther and take a closer look at objects in space.

GALILEO GALILEI
(1564-1642)

CRATERS ON
THE MOON

THE PHASES
OF VENUS

THE MOONS
OF JUPITER

Looking at Jupiter and Venus, an Italian astronomer named **Galileo** found evidence that made it clear the Earth orbits a central Sun (a "**heliocentric**" model). Venus has phases like the Moon— impossible if it orbits the Earth.

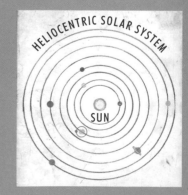

HELIOCENTRIC SOLAR SYSTEM

SUN

In the late 1600s, English scientist **Isaac Newton** discovered why the planets orbit the Sun—a force called **gravity**. He saw an apple fall to the ground and realized that the same force pulling the apple down was pulling the planets in giant loops around the Sun.

A famous story says the apple hit Newton on the head, but it didn't.

TODAY, ASTRONOMERS HAVE BEEN ABLE TO FIND OUT A LOT MORE INFORMATION.

They know that our Sun is just one star out of trillions and trillions in the universe.

They know what it is made of (hydrogen and helium)...

...and how far away it is (93 million miles or 1 Astronomical Unit).

12 astronauts left their footprints on the Moon between 1969 and 1972.

Soon we might send people to Mars for the first time.

WE ALSO KNOW MORE ABOUT THE PLANETS THAN EVER BEFORE.

We have sent machines to explore all eight planets, as well as some of the asteroids, comets, moons, and dwarf planets that also make up the Sun's family of orbiting worlds.

THE SUN

Our Sun is a colossal energy factory constantly churning hydrogen into helium deep in its core. This process creates sunlight, which takes over 100,000 years to make its way through the Sun's layers to reach the surface. From there it takes just over eight minutes to reach Earth.

Astronomers call the Sun a G2V yellow dwarf star.

Most stars are smaller than the Sun, although some are much larger.

You could fit more than 1.3 million Earths inside the Sun (or 1,000 Jupiters).

Dark blemishes are often seen on the surface of the Sun. Astronomers call them **sunspots**. They are simply cooler regions where really intense magnetic activity stops as much heat rising up from inside the Sun. Often appearing in pairs, they are generally bigger than the Earth.

The Sun belches out massive storms into the solar system known as **coronal mass ejections**. A billion tons of material can be spat out at a whopping million miles per hour. They flood the solar system with electrically charged particles that trigger **aurorae** (northern and southern lights) when they reach the planets.

Sometimes our view of the Sun is blocked when the Moon moves directly in the way. Known as a **total solar eclipse**, it casts a shadow onto the Earth. Animals fall silent as the sky darkens, and humans stare up in awe and wonder at this rare event.

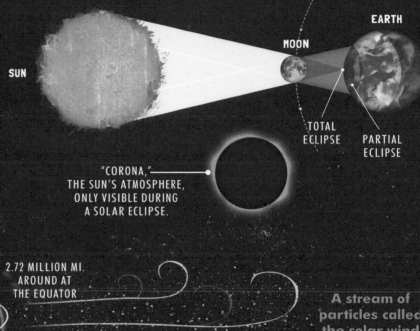

EARTH

MOON

SUN

TOTAL ECLIPSE

PARTIAL ECLIPSE

"CORONA," THE SUN'S ATMOSPHERE, ONLY VISIBLE DURING A SOLAR ECLIPSE.

2.72 MILLION MI. AROUND AT THE EQUATOR

A stream of particles called the solar wind blows outward from the Sun.

You should never look at the Sun without protective equipment.

Nothing lasts forever—even the Sun will eventually die. In around five billion years, it will balloon in size and become a red giant. Mercury and Venus will be swallowed. Earth might be, too. Oceans will boil away and any life left on this planet will be baked to a crisp. The Sun's outer layers will become a planetary nebula as its core forms a white dwarf that'll eventually fade into a black dwarf.

THE LIFE CYCLE OF THE SUN

SUN

RED GIANT

PLANETARY NEBULA

WHITE DWARF

BLACK DWARF

st from the Sun

MERCURY

Day Length	58.65 Earth days
Year Length	87.97 Earth days
Gravity	0.38 of Earth's
Avg. Temperature	332°F
Distance from Sun	0.38 AU
Moons	0

0.1° AXIS

There are records of humans observing Mercury as early as 3,500 years ago.

9,525 MI. AROUND AT THE EQUATOR

WHAT'S INSIDE...

CRUST

MANTLE

SOLID INNER CORE

LIQUID OUTER CORE

The planet's core contains more iron than any other planet.

Occasionally we see Mercury move in front of the Sun in an event called a "transit."

The planet is so close to the Sun, feeling such extreme gravity, that it has probably never had a moon of its own. Instead, the only thing ever to orbit Mercury is the human-made **MESSENGER** space probe sent by NASA to explore the planet between 2011 and 2015.

**MESSENGER
SPACE PROBE**

Isaac Newton's ideas about gravity could explain the behavior of all the planets, except for Mercury. When gravity gets particularly strong—such as where Mercury orbits the Sun—**Albert Einstein's** picture of gravity is more accurate. Einstein's theory of gravity is known as the **General Theory of Relativity**.

$$G\mu v = \frac{8\pi G}{c^4} \, T\mu r$$

Over two orbits of the Sun, Mercury spins three times on its own axis. This pattern, unique to the Sun's closest planet, means that anyone on the surface of Mercury would see a day—the period from one sunrise to the next—last two Mercurian years.

Mercury is the most "eccentric" planet—its orbit is the least circular.

Just a little bit larger than Earth's moon, Mercury is the **smallest** planet in the solar system as well as the closest to the Sun. Its day side is baked to 806°F but, without a thick atmosphere to hold in the heat, night-time temperatures plummet to -274°F.

Mercury has one of the largest impact craters in the solar system—the Caloris Basin. It is over 932 miles across and is surrounded by a ring of mountains 1.2 miles high. The force of the impact sent quakes running in opposite directions around the planet.

THIN ATMOSPHERE CAN'T HOLD THE HEAT IN

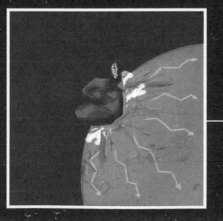

932 MI.

1.2 MI.

Mercury's craters are named after famous artists, writers, and musicians, such as Picasso, Dickens, and Beethoven.

VENUS

Day Length	243 Earth days
Year Length	225 Earth days
Gravity	0.91 of Earth's
Avg. Temperature	869°F
Distance from Sun	0.7 AU
Moons	0

We occasionally see Venus move in front of the Sun, but it won't happen again until 2117.

The planet is named after the Roman goddess of love and beauty.

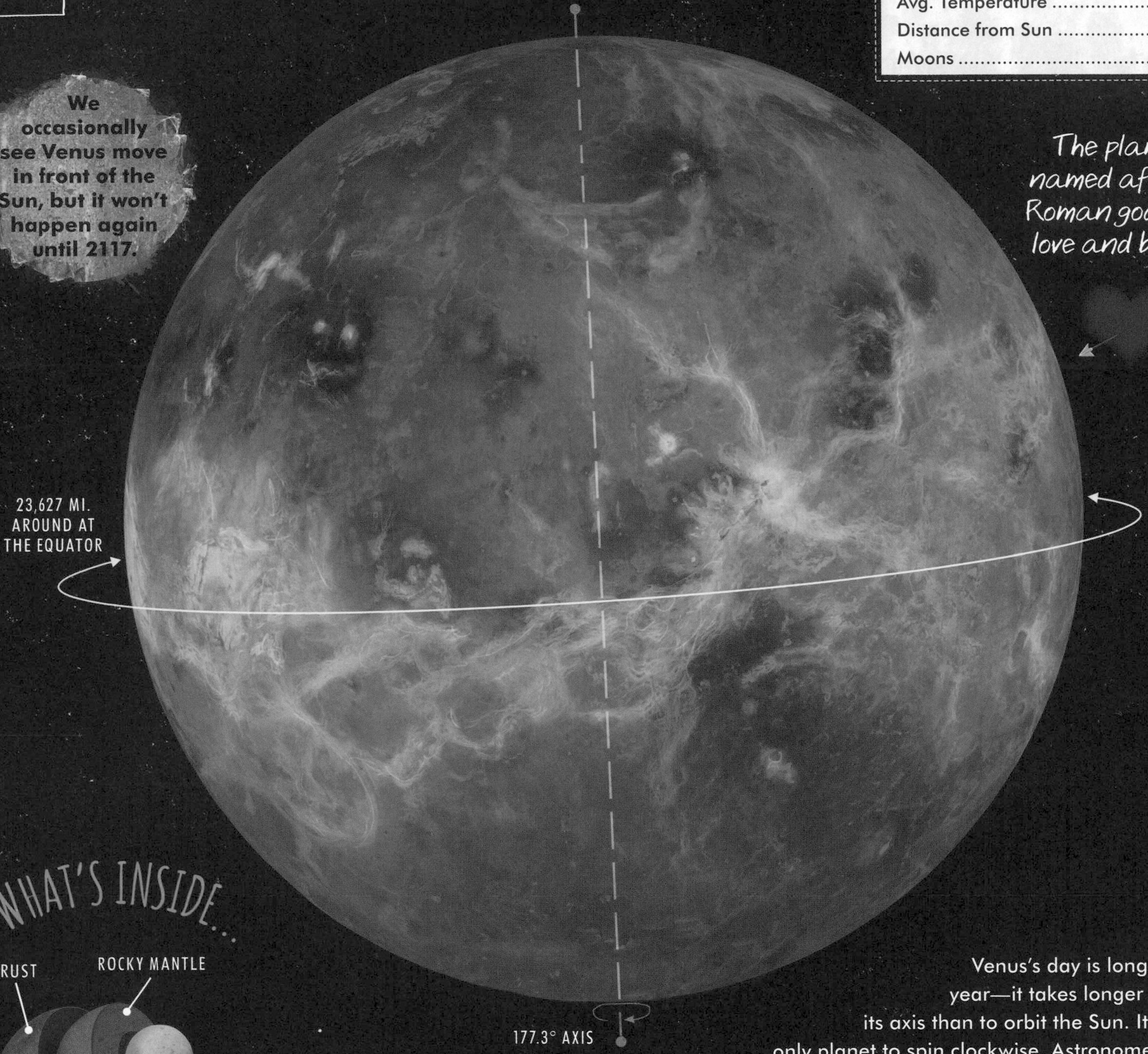

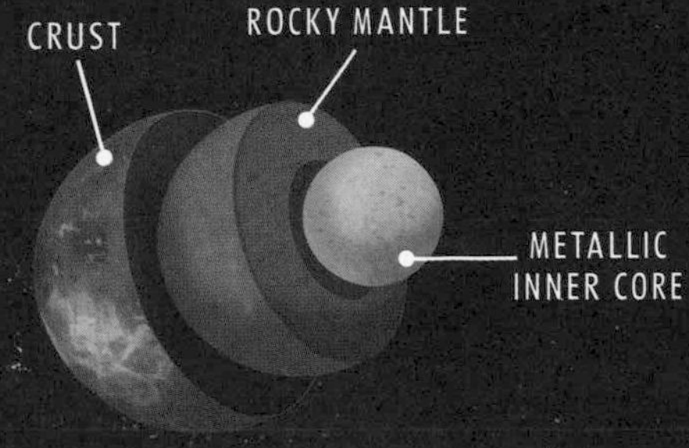

23,627 MI. AROUND AT THE EQUATOR

WHAT'S INSIDE...

CRUST

ROCKY MANTLE

METALLIC INNER CORE

177.3° AXIS

Venus's day is longer than its year—it takes longer to spin on its axis than to orbit the Sun. It's also the only planet to spin clockwise. Astronomers believe it started spinning the same way as its neighbors, but was either turned upside down or its spin changed direction.

Sometimes Venus is called **"Earth's twin,"** but the only similarity is size. Our nearest planetary neighbor is a hellish world with thick carbon dioxide clouds crushing down onto the surface. Not only can temperatures reach 869°F, the air is laced with burning sulfuric acid. *You'd be baked, crushed, and dissolved.*

Despite its unfriendly conditions, we have landed some probes onto Venus's surface. The first—the Soviet Union's **Venera 7** in 1970—managed to hold out for 23 minutes before succumbing to the horrible climate.

VENERA 7

More recently, the **Venus Express** and **Akatsuki** probes have studied the planet from orbit.

VENUS EXPRESS

One way to peer beneath the Venusian clouds is to send **radio waves** down through Venus's atmosphere. If they bounce back quickly, then they have hit something high, perhaps a mountain or volcano. We've discovered the planet's tallest feature is **Maat Mons**, a volcano standing almost as high as Mount Everest here on Earth.

MAAT MONS (5 MI. HIGH)

Winds can whip all the way around the planet in just four days.

REFLECTIVE CLOUDS

With only three exceptions, all craters on Venus are named after women.

Venus's closeness to Earth, along with its highly reflective clouds, makes it the brightest planet in the night sky. Known as both the "morning star" and the "evening star," it can often be seen as a fixed white light hanging close to the ground just before sunrise or just after sunset.

EARTH

Our planet is the only one known to host life. We have plenty of liquid water—a crucial ingredient for living things—because we sit in the perfect warm spot around the Sun. Astronomers call it the **Goldilocks Zone** after the porridge in the fairytale. Not too hot, not too cold—just right.

23.4° AXIS

71% of the Earth's surface is covered in water.

24,901 MI. AROUND AT THE EQUATOR

238,855 MI.

THE MOON (page 22)

WHAT'S INSIDE...

CRUST

MANTLE

SOLID INNER CORE

LIQUID OUTER CORE

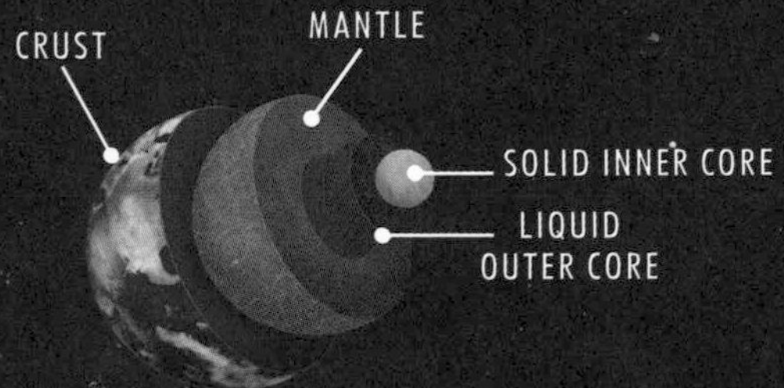

If Earth were an apple, the crust would only be as thick as the skin.

Day Length	24 hours
Year Length	365 days
Gravity	32.2 ft./s²
Avg. Temperature	59°F
Distance from Sun	1 AU
Moons	1

The **atmosphere** above our heads is 78% nitrogen and 21% oxygen, with the other 1% made of small traces of other gases such as carbon dioxide. We need the oxygen to breathe, and the sky is constantly being refilled with it by plants, trees, and microbes in the ocean.

EXOSPHERE — 429 MI.
THERMOSPHERE
KÁRMÁN LINE — 62 MI.
— 53 MI.
MESOSPHERE — 31 MI.
STRATOSPHERE — 12.4 MI.
TROPOSPHERE

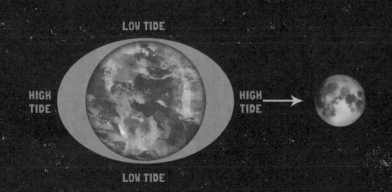

SPRING

WINTER

SUMMER

FALL

We experience changing seasons because the Earth's axis is tilted. It's summer when our half of the planet is titled toward the Sun. Winter comes when we're tipped away. We have the gravity of the Moon to thank for the angle of our axis staying the same. Otherwise the seasons would change wildly.

The Earth's surface is a giant jigsaw puzzle, with pieces called tectonic plates.

LOW TIDE

HIGH TIDE

HIGH TIDE

LOW TIDE

The Moon also plays a big part in the tides. Together with the Sun, it pulls on the Earth and creates a bulge of water on one side of our planet—an area of high tide. The water is pulled away from the top and bottom of the Earth, creating areas of low tide.

Earth is one of only two places in the solar system (along with Jupiter's moon, Io) with active volcanoes. Molten rock breaks through the Earth's crust from a layer underneath called the **mantle**. As this lava cools, it creates huge chains of volcanoes which continue to erupt.

THE MOON

The Moon is the brightest object in the night sky because it's the closest thing to us in space. It doesn't make any light of its own, but rather reflects light from the Sun like a mirror. How much light it reflects toward us depends on its position around the Earth.

6.68° AXIS

Day Length	27.3 Earth days
Year Length	27.3 Earth days
Gravity	0.17 of Earth's
Avg. Temperature	-63.4°F
Distance from Earth	238,855 mi.

Two tortoises flew around the Moon as part of the Soviet Union's 1968 Zond 5 mission.

6,786 MI. AROUND AT THE EQUATOR

All the other planets would fit in the gap between the Earth and the Moon.

WHAT'S INSIDE...

CRUST

MANTLE

INNER CORE

OUTER CORE

238,855 MI.

The Moon is moving away from the Earth by 1.5 in. every year.

Astronomers believe the Moon was formed from the Earth. When our planet was still very young, it got hit by a planet the size of Mars. The calamitous collision sent a lot of debris flying into orbit around the Earth. Gravity collected it together to form the Moon.

As the Moon goes around the Earth, it **waxes** and **wanes** through a series of phases from a **new Moon** to a **full Moon** and back again. Waxing means growing and waning means shrinking. If the Moon is more than half full, it is called **gibbous**.

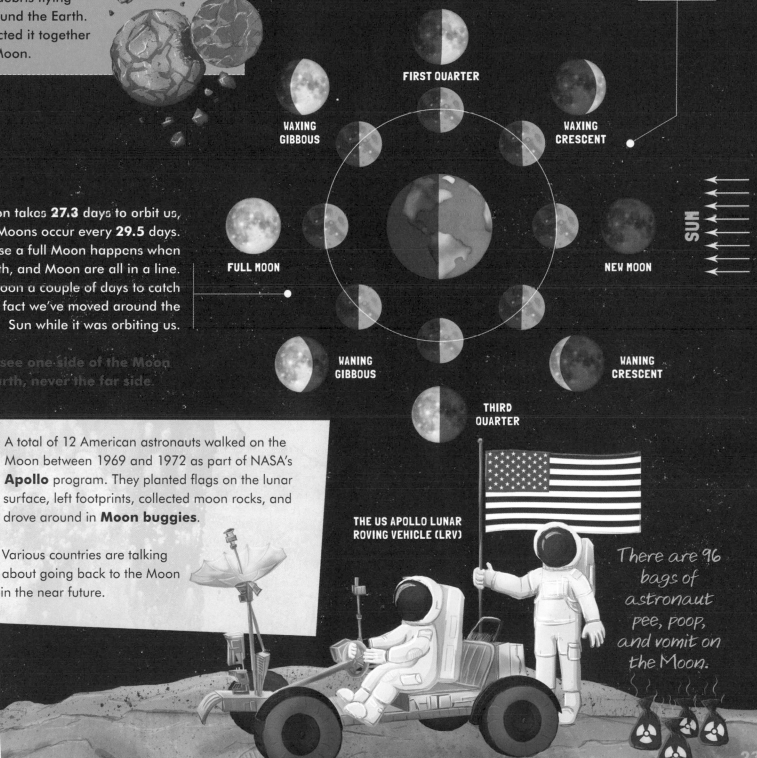

FIRST QUARTER

WAXING GIBBOUS

WAXING CRESCENT

SUN

The Moon takes **27.3** days to orbit us, yet full Moons occur every **29.5** days. That's because a full Moon happens when the Sun, Earth, and Moon are all in a line. It takes the Moon a couple of days to catch up with the fact we've moved around the Sun while it was orbiting us.

FULL MOON

NEW MOON

We only ever see one side of the Moon from the Earth, never the far side.

WANING GIBBOUS

WANING CRESCENT

THIRD QUARTER

A total of 12 American astronauts walked on the Moon between 1969 and 1972 as part of NASA's **Apollo** program. They planted flags on the lunar surface, left footprints, collected moon rocks, and drove around in **Moon buggies**.

Various countries are talking about going back to the Moon in the near future.

THE US APOLLO LUNAR ROVING VEHICLE (LRV)

There are 96 bags of astronaut pee, poop, and vomit on the Moon.

 **MARS**

Day Length	24 hrs 37 mins
Year Length	687 Earth days
Gravity	0.38 of Earth's
Avg. Temperature	-76°F
Distance from Sun	1.5 AU
Moons	2

PHOBOS: 13.7 MI. DIAMETER

25° AXIS

Mars is red because the iron in its rocks has turned to rust.

5,827 MI.

13,262 MI. AROUND AT THE EQUATOR

14,577 MI.

DEIMOS: 7.5 MI. DIAMETER

WHAT'S INSIDE...

CRUST
MANTLE
INNER CORE

Mars has two moons—**Phobos** and **Deimos**. Both are very small, just tens of miles across. That's the size of a city. Phobos is gradually spiraling inward and, in around 30 million years' time, Mars's gravity will rip it into pieces to form a ring around the Red Planet.

**MARINER 9
(NASA 1971)**

**PATHFINDER AND
SOJOURNER
(NASA 1997)**

**MARS EXPRESS
(ESA 2003)**

**MARINER 4
(NASA 1965)**

Mars is the most explored planet in the solar system. We have sent many machines to orbit around, land on, and drive around it. They have shown us that Mars is a very different planet from the Earth—a cold, dry, and dusty desert with no liquid water.

We have a better map of the Martian surface than we do of Earth's ocean floor.

The first person who will walk on Mars is probably alive today. In all likelihood, they are currently in school. That's because the first crew might travel to Mars in a few decades' time. It could be you! Imagine commanding the first human mission to set foot on another planet.

**OPPORTUNITY
(NASA 2004)**

Opportunity (NASA 2004) was designed to last just 90 days, but it's been exploring for over 14 years.

The Red Planet is home to some of the most impressive features in the solar system. The mighty **Olympus Mons** volcano towers over 72,000 feet above the dry Martian surface. A huge canyon system called the **Valles Marineris** cuts almost a quarter of the way around the equator.

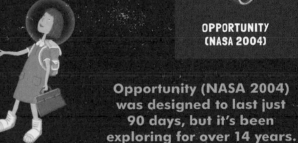

OLYMPUS MONS
72,178 FT.

MT. EVEREST
29,029 FT.

It can snow frozen carbon dioxide on some parts of Mars.

Maybe Mars wasn't always so hostile to life. There is growing evidence that it was once a very different planet with a much thicker atmosphere, and oceans covering at least a fifth of its surface. Astronomers are still trying to figure out why the Martian climate changed so dramatically.

Dust storms the size of continents can cover vast areas of Mars.

JUPITER

3.1° AXIS

NORTHERN LIGHTS

Day Length	9 hrs 50 mins
Year Length	11.86 Earth years
Gravity	2.52 of Earth's
Avg. Temperature	-162.4°F
Distance from Sun	5.2 AU
Moons	69

JUNO SATELLITE

NASA's Juno mission carried three aluminum Lego figures to Jupiter.

Northern and southern lights (aurorae) have been observed on Jupiter.

Big planets close to their stars are known as "hot Jupiters."

272,946 MI. AROUND AT THE EQUATOR

You could fit all of the other planets inside Jupiter.

WHAT'S INSIDE...

HYDROGEN ATMOSPHERE

LIQUID HYDROGEN

ICE AND ROCK INNER CORE

METALLIC HYDROGEN

SOUTHERN LIGHTS

We don't know if Jupiter is a friend or foe. It definitely soaks up some of the **asteroids** and **comets** that might have come dangerously close to Earth. In 1992, Jupiter broke a comet in 23 pieces that would hit and bruise the planet two years later. However, its presence might also nudge some objects in our direction.

Jupiter has the shortest day of any planet—just 9 hours and 50 minutes.

Although its neighbor Saturn is most famous for having rings, Jupiter has them too. Faint and dusty, they were only discovered when the **Voyager 1** space probe flew close to the planet at the end of the 1970s. A lot of the dust comes from some of Jupiter's smaller moons.

The biggest storm on Jupiter is called "**The Great Red Spot**," although it is not as great as it used to be. At one point you could fit four Earths inside. Now it is more like two and a half. Astronomers are still trying to figure out why it is shrinking.

Even through a small telescope you'll see Jupiter's surface is split into different colored bands called "**equatorial belts**." Hidden in these stripes are huge storms where winds can rage at 400 miles per hour. It is also noticeably fatter at the equator because it bulges outward as it spins.

JUPITER'S MOONS

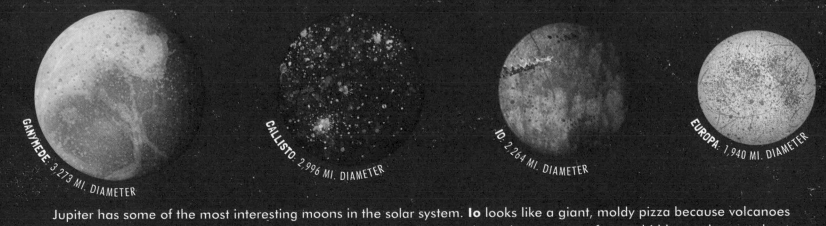

GANYMEDE: 3,273 MI. DIAMETER

CALLISTO: 2,996 MI. DIAMETER

IO: 2,264 MI. DIAMETER

EUROPA: 1,940 MI. DIAMETER

Jupiter has some of the most interesting moons in the solar system. **Io** looks like a giant, moldy pizza because volcanoes are constantly spewing sulfur onto the surface. Its neighbor, **Europa**, has a huge ocean of water hidden under vast sheets of ice. **Ganymede** is the biggest moon in the solar system.

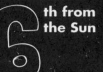

The second biggest planet, Saturn is 764 times bigger than Earth.

SATURN

CASSINI

26.7° AXIS

Day Length	10 hrs 42 mins
Year Length	29.5 Earth years
Gravity	1.07 of Earth's
Avg. Temperature	-218°F
Distance from Sun	9.6 AU
Moons	62

Saturday takes its name from the planet—SATURnDAY

235,298 MI. AROUND AT THE EQUATOR

In recent years we've learned a lot about Saturn thanks to NASA's **Cassini** space probe. It was launched in **1997** and spent a staggering seven years traveling all the way out to Saturn. It stayed there until **2017**, carefully measuring and photographing the planet to help astronomers understand it.

WHAT'S INSIDE...

ATMOSPHERE
GASEOUS HYDROGEN
METALLIC HYDROGEN
ROCKY CORE
LIQUID HYDROGEN

You don't need a space probe to see Saturn for yourself. Even a small telescope would show you the planet as a round yellow circle with rings appearing as a line running through the middle. You can even see Saturn in the sky without a telescope (although not its rings).

Saturn's density is lower than water, meaning it would float in a bathtub.

Jupiter and Saturn make up **92% of the planets' mass.**

Saturn's famous rings may look solid, but they're actually made of individual **ice chunks** that are each about the size of a house. No one knows exactly where they came from, but gather all the pieces together and you'd have something as big as one of Saturn's moons. Maybe an old moon got smashed to bits.

Some astronomers believe that it rains diamonds inside Saturn's atmosphere.

ICE CHUNKS

Astronomers have spotted a giant **hexagonal storm** raging at Saturn's North Pole that's twice as wide as the Earth! Back in 2012 it appeared blue, but several years later it shifted to a more golden color. Winds in the storm can blow at over 185 miles per hour.

SATURN'S MOONS

TITAN: 3,200 MI. DIAMETER

RHEA: 951 MI. DIAMETER

IAPETUS: 907 MI. DIAMETER

DIONE: 696 MI. DIAMETER

TETHYS: 659 MI. DIAMETER

MIMAS: 244 MI. DIAMETER

Saturn has some of the most impressive moons in the solar system. Its largest—**Titan**—is bigger than the planet Mercury and is the only satellite in the solar system with a thick atmosphere. Space scientists landed the **Huygens probe** on its icy surface in January **2005**.

URANUS

The seventh planet orbits the Sun on its side—its axis is tipped over by more than ninety degrees. That means that for half of Uranus's 84-year orbit, one pole is constantly in the dark. For the other 42 years it is constantly lit up.

Uranus's might be askew because a giant impact knocked it over.

Day Length	17 hrs 14 mins
Year Length	84 Earth years
Gravity	0.89 of Earth's
Avg. Temperature	-322°F
Distance from Sun	19 AU
Moons	27

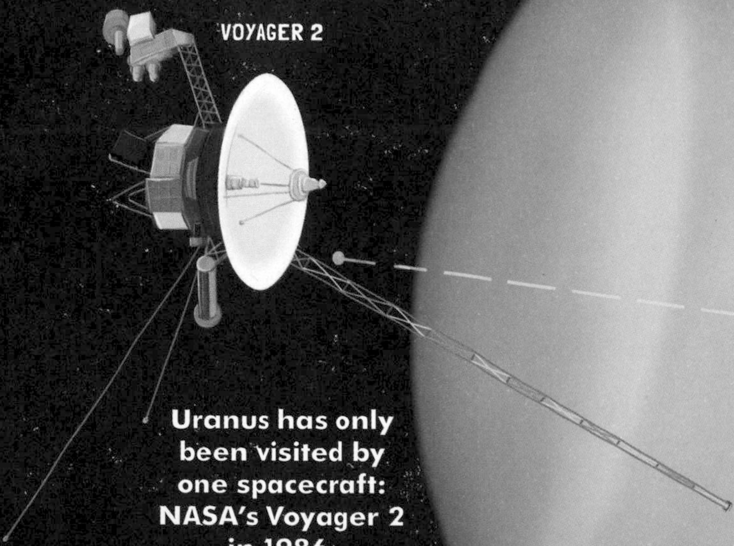

VOYAGER 2

Uranus has only been visited by one spacecraft: NASA's Voyager 2 in 1986.

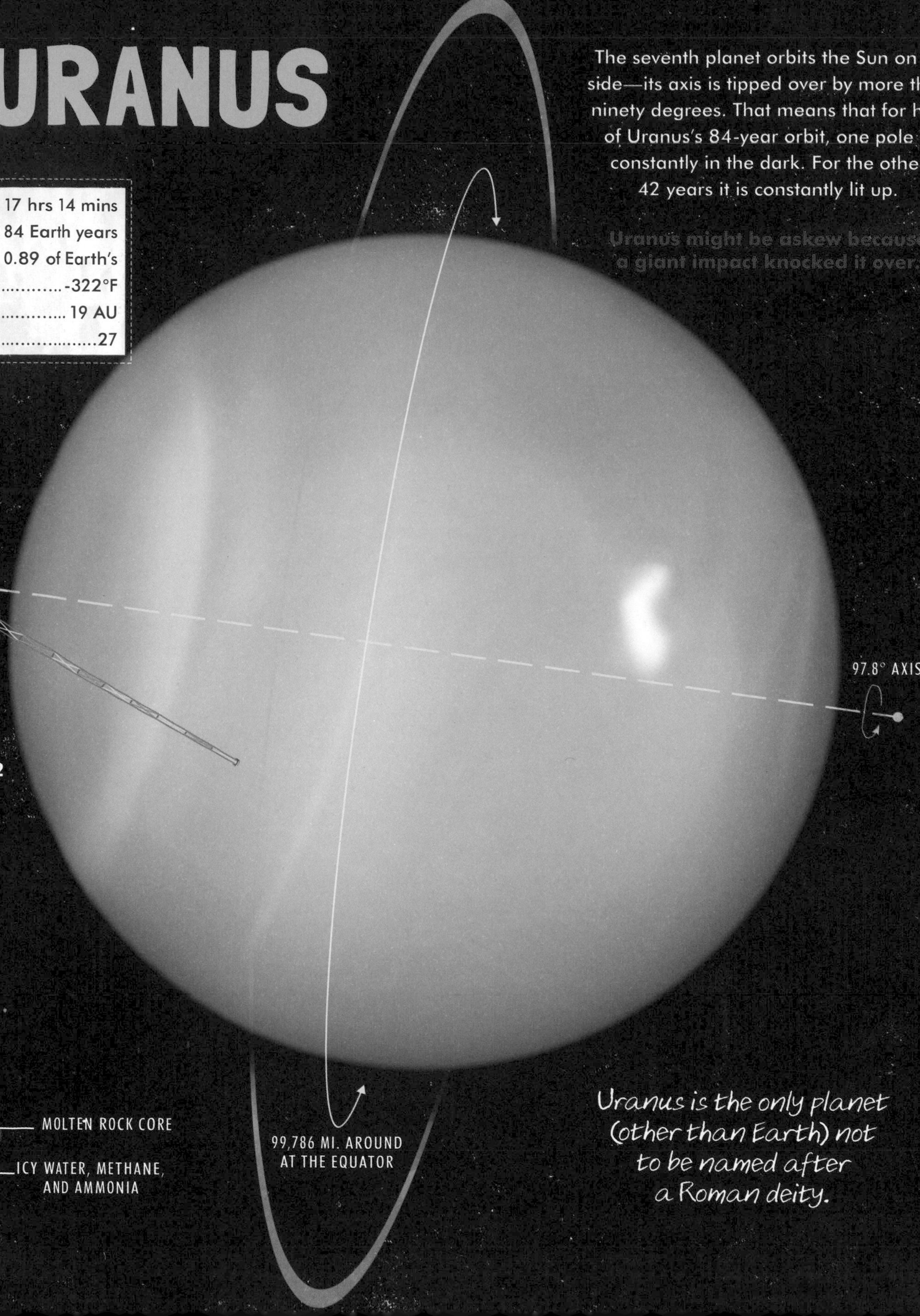

97.8° AXIS

WHAT'S INSIDE...

GAS ATMOSPHERE

LIQUID HYDROGEN

MOLTEN ROCK CORE

ICY WATER, METHANE, AND AMMONIA

99,786 MI. AROUND AT THE EQUATOR

Uranus is the only planet (other than Earth) not to be named after a Roman deity.

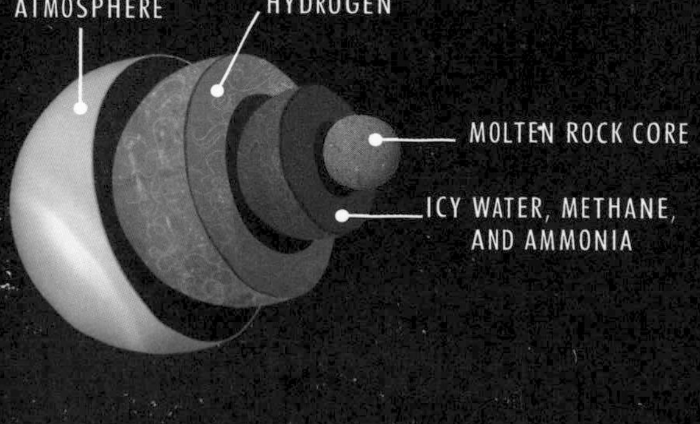

Uranus was the **first planet** ever to be discovered. Mercury, Venus, Mars, Jupiter, and Saturn can all easily be seen with your eyes, but for Uranus, it helps to have a **telescope**.

British astronomer **William Herschel** found Uranus using his telescope at home on March 13, 1781.

Herschel originally called the planet "George's Star" after King George III.

Uranus has a distinctive **light-blue** appearance, but it is not made of water. Instead, **methane gas** in its atmosphere absorbs a lot of the red light hitting the planet. With the red light removed, the light it reflects out toward us is mostly blue.

Like all the giant planets, Uranus has a **ring system**. It is made of dark particles, each less than 3 feet across. Astronomers have spotted a total of 13 rings around Uranus. They are thought to be less than 600 million years old, and the first was discovered in 1977.

The sunlight on Uranus is only 0.25% as strong as sunlight on Earth.

URANUS'S MOONS

Uranus has 27 known moons, all named after famous characters from stories by William Shakespeare or Alexander Pope, including **Romeo**, **Juliet**, and **Puck**. **Miranda** is one of the oddest moons because it looks like it has been broken apart and put back together again. **Titania** is the biggest Uranian moon.

TITANIA: 981 MI. DIAMETER

OBERON: 946 MI. DIAMETER

UMBRIEL: 726 MI. DIAMETER

ARIEL: 719 MI. DIAMETER

MIRANDA: 293 MI. DIAMETER

PUCK: 101 MI. DIAMETER

NEPTUNE

Day Length	16 hrs 6 mins
Year Length	165 Earth years
Gravity	1.12 of Earth's
Avg. Temperature	-330°F
Distance from Sun	30 AU
Moons	14

28.3° AXIS

Other names considered for Neptune included Janus and Oceanus.

Neptune is named after the Roman god of the sea.

96,685 MI. AROUND AT THE EQUATOR

VOYAGER 2

WHAT'S INSIDE...

GAS ATMOSPHERE

FROZEN WATER, AMMONIA, AND METHANE

SOLID ROCK AND ICE CORE

It takes Neptune **165 years** to make one lap of the Sun because it sits so far out. The **Voyager 2** space probe took 12 years to make it all the way out there. Even light from the Sun takes over four hours to make the journey (it takes just over eight minutes to reach Earth).

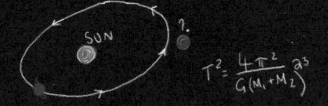

$$T^2 = \frac{4\pi^2}{G(M_1 + M_2)} a^3$$

Neptune was predicted to exist by astronomers before they found it in 1846. They noticed Uranus speeding up and slowing down in its journey around the Sun and correctly guessed that was because an eighth planet was pulling on it with its gravity. They then used math to work out where it was.

Galileo saw Neptune in 1612 and 1613, but didn't realize it was a planet.

NEPTUNE'S MOONS

There are **14** known Neptunian moons, with the last discovered as recently as 2013. The largest—**Triton**—orbits Neptune in the opposite direction of the spin of the planet. This is probably because it was an object Neptune dragged in from the Kuiper Belt.

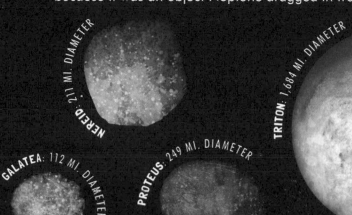

NEREID: 211 MI. DIAMETER

TRITON: 1,684 MI. DIAMETER

GALATEA: 112 MI. DIAMETER

PROTEUS: 249 MI. DIAMETER

ADAMS   ARAGO

LASSELL

LE VERRIER

GALLE

Neptune has five main rings, all named after people who played an important role in the discovery of the planet: **Galle**, **Le Verrier**, **Lassell**, **Arago**, and **Adams**. There are 42 wiggles in the Adams ring, each 18.6 miles in size, caused by the gravity of the moon Galatea.

Neptune is the densest of the four giant planets.

The furthest confirmed planet from the Sun, Neptune has the strongest winds in the solar system—they can blow at over 1,200 miles per hour, around 17 times stronger than a hurricane on Earth. A huge storm known as the Great Dark Spot was seen in 1989, but by 1994 it had disappeared.

DWARF PLANETS

Just what separates a planet from everything else orbiting the Sun? The list of planets has already changed many times. When the asteroid Ceres was discovered in 1801, it was called a planet, before being removed from the list decades later. Pluto, too, was said to be a planet when it was found in 1930.

Astronomers finally wrote a list of things a planet should be or do in 2006. It has to **orbit the Sun** and be **round** in shape. Most importantly, it has to have "cleared the neighborhood around its orbit." In other words, it has to be the gravitational boss of its journey around the Sun.

Pluto is not the boss of its orbit because it crosses orbits with something bigger—Neptune. It is also greatly affected by Neptune's gravity. So astronomers invented a new term for objects like Pluto: **dwarf planet**. Four other objects (including **Ceres**) are also now classified as dwarf planets.

Ceres has two bright white spots that continue to puzzle astronomers.

PLUTO

NEPTUNE

SUN

PLUTO

39.5 AU FROM THE SUN

Diameter .... 1,478 mi.
Day Length ....6.4 Earth days
Year Length ....248 Earth years
Avg. Temperature .... -387°F
Moons 5

FROZEN METHANE NITROGEN CRUST

WATER AND ICE MANTLE

SOLID ROCK CORE

CHARON

Charon has places called Gallifrey Macula and Tardis Chasma after The Doctor's home planet and time-machine in the TV series *Dr Who.*

PLUTO

NIX

STYX

KERBEROS

119.5° AXIS

HYDRA

MAKEMAKE

Diameter ....901 mi.

Day Length .... 22 hrs 30 mins

Year Length ....309 Earth years

Avg. Temperature ....-400°F

Moons 1

Makemake was found at Easter and so was known as "Easter bunny."

MAKEMAKE

S/2015 (136472) 1

ERIS

ERIS

Diameter .... 1,445 mi.

Day Length ....25 hrs 54 mins

Year Length ....557 Earth years

Avg. Temperature ....-400°F

Moons 1

Eris sits beyond the Kuiper Belt in a region called The Scattered Disc.

DYSNOMIA

HI'IAKA

NAMAKA

HAUMEA

HAUMEA

Diameter .... 1,014 mi.

Day Length .... 3 hrs 54 mins

Year Length .... 285 Earth years

Avg. Temperature ....-402°F

Moons 2

Haumea was found at Christmas, so was nicknamed "Santa."

NASA's **New Horizons** probe was launched in **2006** and finally arrived at **Pluto** in **2015**, where it took the first up-close images of this cold little world. It is continuing to journey farther into the Kuiper Belt to explore more of the outer solar system.

There are almost certainly more than five dwarf planets. Other objects orbiting the Sun, like **Sedna** and **Orcus**, will probably be added to the list one day. However, we have to wait until we have good enough telescopes to prove that they are round in shape.

ASTEROIDS

Asteroids are leftover building blocks from the formation of the rocky planets. Most of the rocks there have been kicked out over time, and today the whole Asteroid Belt weighs just 4% of the Moon (or less than 25% of Pluto). They range from 590 miles across to the size of dust and pebbles.

VESTA: 329 MI. DIAMETER

CERES: 590 MI. DIAMETER

NASA's Dawn mission visited two asteroids— Vesta and Ceres.

DAWN SATELLITE

ASTEROID BELT

KUIPER BELT

PALLAS: 339 MI. DIAMETER

Astronomers keep a close eye on asteroids because they can be dangerous. 66 million years ago an asteroid the size of a city hit the coast of Mexico, wiping out the **dinosaurs** and killing off more than 70% of all life on Earth. Today we'd see it coming.

HYGIEA: 276 MI. DIAMETER

A 66-foot asteroid tore through the sky over Russia in 2013, shattering windows.

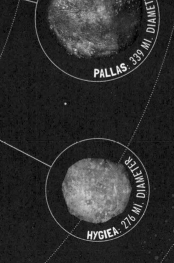

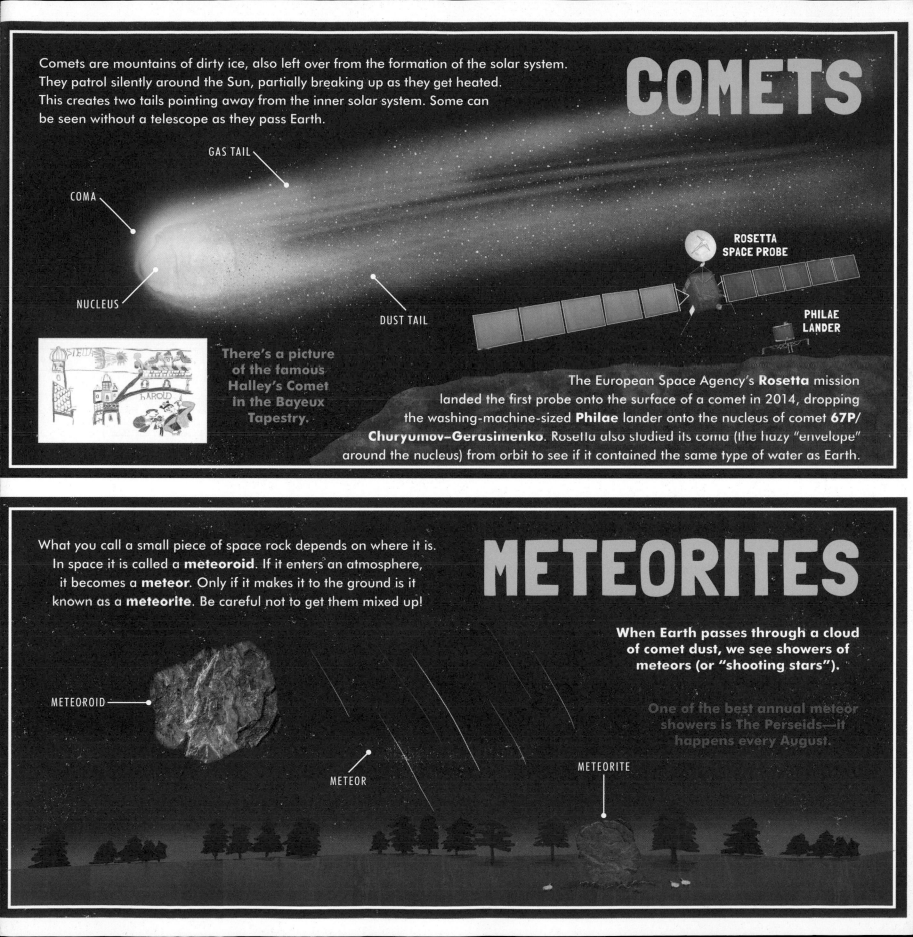

COMETS

Comets are mountains of dirty ice, also left over from the formation of the solar system. They patrol silently around the Sun, partially breaking up as they get heated. This creates two tails pointing away from the inner solar system. Some can be seen without a telescope as they pass Earth.

GAS TAIL

COMA

NUCLEUS

DUST TAIL

ROSETTA SPACE PROBE

PHILAE LANDER

There's a picture of the famous Halley's Comet In the Bayeux Tapestry.

The European Space Agency's **Rosetta** mission landed the first probe onto the surface of a comet in 2014, dropping the washing-machine-sized **Philae** lander onto the nucleus of comet **67P/Churyumov–Gerasimenko**. Rosetta also studied its coma (the hazy "envelope" around the nucleus) from orbit to see if it contained the same type of water as Earth.

METEORITES

What you call a small piece of space rock depends on where it is. In space it is called a **meteoroid**. If it enters an atmosphere, it becomes a **meteor**. Only if it makes it to the ground is it known as a **meteorite**. Be careful not to get them mixed up!

When Earth passes through a cloud of comet dust, we see showers of meteors (or "shooting stars").

One of the best annual meteor showers is The Perseids—it happens every August.

METEOROID

METEOR

METEORITE

THE SPACE RACE

MARINER 2

V-2 ROCKET

YURI GAGARIN

1897
Russian scientist **Konstantin Tsiolkovsky** figured out the science of rockets in **1897**.

1942
The **V-2 rocket** was the first to cross the Kármán line—the boundary that marks the beginning of outer space—in **1942**.

1962
The **Mariner 2** space probe was the first successful interplanetary spacecraft, in **1962**.

The first woman in space was Soviet cosmonaut **Valentina Tereshkova**, in 1963.

CCCP

VALENTINA TERESHKOVA

1961
The Soviets were the first to put a person in space. On **April 12, 1961**, cosmonaut **Yuri Gagarin** orbited the Earth once before landing in the middle of a field close to a farmer and his daughter. Yuri became an instant, worldwide celebrity.

1963
In recent years, space exploration has been more of a joint effort between many countries working together. The **International Space Station** is home to a multinational crew of astronauts sharing knowledge about how best to work in space. They are learning how to survive in space for long periods of time.

VOYAGER 1

INTERNATIONAL SPACE STATION

1998

2012
In **2012**, the **Voyager 1** probe entered interstellar space.

In **2014**, the European Space Agency's **Rosetta** probe made a historic landing on a comet, dropping the **Philae** lander onto the nucleus.

ROSETTA PROBE

PHILAE LANDER

SPACE LETTUCE

In **2015**, lettuce became the first food to be grown in space.

2014

2015

The first animals in space were fruit flies, launched by the U.S. in **1947**.

SPACE FLIES

1947

ALBERT II

1949

Albert II became the first monkey in space, in **1949**.

SPUTNIK 1

In **1959**, **Luna 2** became the first spacecraft to reach the surface of the Moon.

LUNA 2

In **1957**, the Soviet Union sent **Sputnik 1** into space—the first human-made object to orbit the Earth. It stayed in orbit for three months before burning up in the atmosphere. It sent out a series of radio beeps so that it could be tracked from the ground.

1957

1959

Cosmonaut **Alexei Leonov** performed the first space walk in **1965**.

ALEXEI LEONOV

The Americans finally achieved an important first in space exploration when they successfully landed people on the Moon in July **1969**. **Neil Armstrong** stepped off the ladder of the landing module and uttered the famous words "It's one small step for [a] man, one giant leap for mankind."

1969

1965

Discovery (OV-103) was NASA's third space shuttle orbiter and made its first mission in **1984**. It would go on to complete over 30 missions, more than any other orbiter.

NEIL ARMSTRONG

DISCOVERY

SPACEX FALCON HEAVY ROCKET

In **2018**, **SpaceX** founder Elon Musk launched his red sports car into space on the **Falcon Heavy** rocket.

1984

2018

SPACE ROCKETS

Space is only 62 miles above your head, but getting there is really difficult because **gravity** tries to keep you stuck to the ground. To get away from Earth you need to travel at **"escape velocity,"** which is **7 miles per second**—faster than a speeding bullet.

To reach escape velocity, we humans have built many different rockets. They work by burning liquid fuel and directing hot gas out of nozzles at the bottom. This sends them roaring into the sky.

Often rockets are built from many parts—or stages—that separate in flight.

A new rocket called the Falcon Heavy is the biggest since the Saturn V.

The most powerful rocket of all time was the mighty **Saturn V**, which carried the Apollo astronauts to the Moon. It is also the tallest and heaviest rocket used so far. It burned through 22 tons of fuel every second, and each launch cost over $1 billion in today's money.

164 FT.

SOYUZ (OKB-1)

184 FT.

SHUTTLE DISCOVERY (NASA)

193 FT.

ARIANE 4 (ESA)

230 FT.

FALCON HEAVY

363 FT.

SATURN V

3RD STAGE: S-IVB

2ND STAGE: S-II

1ST STAGE: S-IC

LIQUID NITROGEN

LIQUID OXYGEN

APOLLO MODULE

LUNAR MODULE

ESCAPE ROCKET

3RD STAGE: S-IVB

INTERSTAGE ADAPTER

LIQUID HYDROGEN

LIQUID OXYGEN

2ND STAGE: S-II

BOOSTERS

LIQUID OXYGEN

KEROSENE

1ST STAGE: S-IC

4. 2ND STAGE SEPARATION (5 MINUTES)

124 MI.

106 MI.

5. 3RD STAGE SEPARATION (9 MINUTES)

CAPSULE OPENS
FOR JOURNEY AND
DOCKING

THERMOSPHERE
50–435 MI.

6. TIME IN ORBIT

3. FAIRING JETTISONED (3 MINUTES)

Fewer than 600 people have ever launched into space. Only 24 astronauts have left Low-Earth Orbit (LEO).

TO SPACE AND BACK IN A SOYUZ ROCKET

7. RETURN TO EARTH

KÁRMÁN LINE

Astronauts visiting the International Space Station currently travel in Soyuz rockets.

KÁRMÁN LINE

62 MI.

62 MI.

PARTS BURN UP IN ATMOSPHERE

2. BOOSTERS SEPARATION (2 MINUTES)

Re-entering Earth's atmosphere at the end of a mission is just as dangerous as launching into space in the first place. Friction with the air heats the outside of the capsule to 3,632°F. The angle of approach is crucial—too steep and you'll burn up completely.

MESOSPHERE
31–50 MI.

3 HOURS TO RETURN TO EARTH

25 MI.

It's a tradition for astronauts launching from Kazakhstan to pee on the tire of their bus!

STRATOSPHERE
7.5–31 MI.

1. TAKEOFF (12 SECONDS)

As the Soyuz capsule approaches the ground, parachutes are deployed to slow you down. However, you still hit the ground with a mighty bump. Helicopters land nearby with a rescue team to help you out of the capsule as you get used to gravity again after months of weightlessness in space.

8. TOUCHDOWN

TROPOSPHERE
0–7.5 MI.

EXPLORATION

We have sent machines to every planet in the solar system, along with some of their moons, as well as asteroids, comets, and dwarf planets.

FLYBY

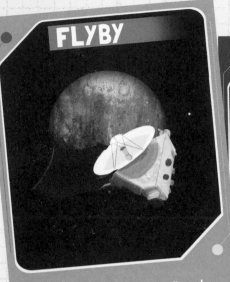

Sometimes the machine flew by...

ORBITER

...and other times it went into orbit as an artificial moon.

LANDER

Landers and...

ROVER

...rovers can explore worlds with solid surfaces.

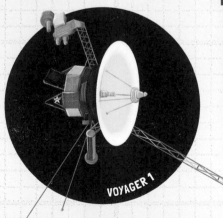

Voyager 1 is the farthest probe from Earth—currently 13 billion miles away.

Sending machines is a lot easier than sending people. The weight of the mission is lighter, and so it's cheaper. Robots don't need food, water, or oxygen and if the probe accidentally crashes, then nobody is hurt. They also allow us to learn about a place before considering whether to send astronauts there.

Rovers have explored both the surface of the Moon and Mars.

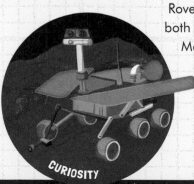

CURIOSITY

VENERA 3

In 1966, the Soviet **Venera 3** probe became the first human-made object to touch another planet's surface.

Scientists are already talking about the possibility of sending the first machines out of the solar system to visit another star. A swarm of tiny computer chips could be fired there using laser beams beamed into space from the Earth's surface...

OSIRIS-REX

BENNU

In the near future, missions will look into the possibility of mining asteroids for their precious metals. **Satellites** have already been launched to identify the best targets.

NASA's **OSIRIS-REx** is currently exploring the asteroid **Bennu** and will bring a sample back to the Earth in **2023**.

Jupiter's moon, **Europa**, is one of the most exciting places in the solar system to explore for signs of life because it is thought to host an ocean of liquid water.

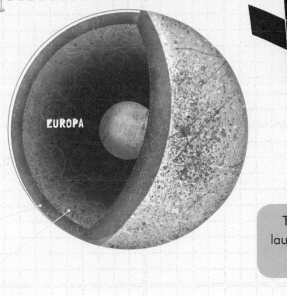

EUROPA

ICY CRUST

OCEAN

MANTLE

JUPITER ICY MOONS EXPLORER (JUICE)

The European Space Agency plans to launch the **Jupiter Icy Moons Explorer** (**JUICE**) in **2022** for a closer look.

CHANG'E-5

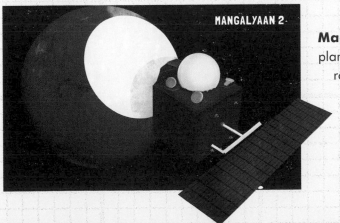

MANGALYAAN 2

Mangalyaan 2 is a planned Indian Mars rover mission in the 2020s.

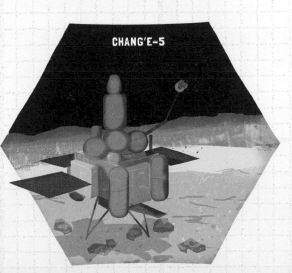

The Chinese Space Agency is hoping to send robots to bring moon rocks home.

...The journey would take a staggering 40 years.

INTERNATIONAL SPACE STATION

The International Space Station is a home for humanity in orbit. It has been permanently inhabited by astronauts since November 2000. Crew members typically spend six months on board, although some have stayed as long as a year. They help us understand the effects long stays in space have on the human body.

Liquid salt and pepper are used— granules could go into astronauts' eyes.

LABORATORY MODULE

ZARYA SERVICE MODULE

PIERS DOCKING PORT

DOCKING & CARGO PORT

CANADARM2

QUEST AIRLOCK

KIBO RESEARCH MODULE

HARMONY NODE

KIBO OUTER RESEARCH PLATFORM

Astronauts on the ISS sleep inside sleeping bags tied to the wall.

Crew members see 16 sunsets and sunrises every single day.

The **solar panels** on the ISS are so reflective that you can easily see it from the ground at night. Brighter than any of the planets, it is not above you for very long, though. Orbiting the whole planet in just 92 minutes, it soon disappears from view.

Astronauts aboard the ISS float around because they are weightless. However, this does not mean there is no gravity in space. If that were true, then there'd be nothing stopping the Space Station from floating off into the solar system. Astronauts float because they are in freefall around the planet.

EXPLORING SPACE
WITHOUT A ROCKET

Telescopes allow us to see fainter objects farther away in space. They also provide a stunning closer look at familiar objects like the Moon. Professional astronomers have built enormous telescopes on the tops of mountains and launched others into space, all to learn more about how the universe works.

HUBBLE TELESCOPE

You don't need a mega telescope to see wondrous things in the night sky. Even a small one will show you craters on the Moon, the moons of Jupiter, and the rings of Saturn.

Some telescopes view space using other forms of light, such as radio waves or X-rays.

Nothing beats seeing these things for yourself! Binoculars, too, can be a great way to explore the sky.

The biggest telescopes in the world have mirrors around 33 feet across.

45

GLOSSARY

Astronaut Buzz Aldrin

asteroid a small chunk of rock and/or metal left over from the formation of the solar system

asteroid belt a collection of rocky and metallic objects between Mars and Jupiter left over from the formation of the solar system

astronaut a person who has traveled into space

astronomer a person whose job it is to study space

astronomical unit (AU) the distance of the Earth from the Sun

atmosphere the layers of gas surrounding a planet or moon

atom the tiny building blocks from which everything around us is made

axis the imaginary line around which an object spins

black dwarf what a white dwarf becomes as it cools and fades

comet a chunk of ice in the solar system left over from its formation

coronal mass ejection a huge eruption of hot gas from the Sun

cosmonaut the Russian word for an astronaut

Cosmonaut Valentina Tereshkova

crust the outer layer of a rocky planet, moon, or asteroid

dark energy the mysterious substance thought to be making the expansion of the universe speed up

dark matter an invisible "glue" thought to help bind galaxies and clusters of galaxies together

dark particle the particles of which dark matter is thought to consist

dark spot a dull, stormy region on the surface of a gas planet such as Neptune

density how much material is packed into a given amount of space

dwarf planet a round object orbiting the Sun that hasn't cleared the path of that orbit

energy the capacity to do work

The **International Space Station (ISS)**

equator the imaginary line running around the middle of a planet or moon

fairing equipment used to protect spacecraft from aerodynamic forces shortly after takeoff

galaxy a huge collection of billions of stars all stuck together by gravity

galaxy cluster a group of galaxies

gas cloud a collection of gas and dust in space

gravity the attractive force between two or more objects with mass

ice line an imaginary line in the solar system after which the temperature drops to below freezing

International Space Station (ISS) an inhabited spacecraft orbiting around the Earth

A **comet**

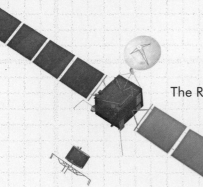

The Rosetta **space probe**

The Philae **lander**

Curiosity, a Mars **rover**

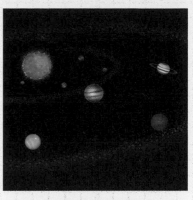

The **solar system**

Kuiper Belt a collection of small objects orbiting the Sun beyond Neptune

lander a machine sent to touch down on another planet or moon

Low-Earth Orbit (LEO) the region of space that is closest to the Earth

mantle the layer just below a planet's crust

meteor a piece of space debris moving through the atmosphere

meteorite a piece of space debris that makes it to the Earth's surface

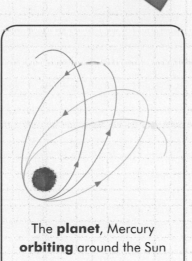

The **planet**, Mercury **orbiting** around the Sun

meteoroid a piece of natural debris still in space

Milky Way our galaxy

moon a naturally occurring object that orbits around a planet

orbit the path an object in space takes around another

particle a tiny piece of matter

phase the apparent shape of an object depending on how it is lit up

planet a round object orbiting the Sun that has cleared the path of its orbit of small things

planetary nebula the colorful gas cloud surrounding a star like the Sun when it dies

red giant what a star like the Sun becomes when it gets bigger as it starts to die

ring a flat band of tiny objects orbiting a planet

rover a machine sent to another world to drive on its surface

satellite an object orbiting another in space

solar system the Sun's family of orbiting worlds

space probe a machine sent into space to explore

star a big ball of gas in space that makes its own light

sunspot a dark patch on the Sun

universe everything that exists

white dwarf the remaining core of a dying Sun-like star

white spot a bright area on the surface of an object, such as Ceres

Our **galaxy**, the **Milky Way**

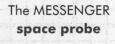

The MESSENGER **space probe**

Colin Stuart is a Fellow of the Royal Astronomical Society, an astronomy speaker, and author who has talked to well over a quarter of a million people about the universe, ranging from schools and the public to conferences and businesses. His books have sold more than 150,000 copies worldwide and he's written over 150 popular science articles for publications including *The Guardian*, *New Scientist*, *BBC Focus,* and the *European Space Agency*. In recognition of his efforts to popularize astronomy, the asteroid (15347) Colinstuart is named after him. www.colinstuart.net

Button
BOOKS

First published 2019 by Button Books, an imprint of Guild of Master Craftsman Publications Ltd, Castle Place, 166 High Street, Lewes, East Sussex BN7 1XU, UK. Text © Colin Stuart, 2019. Illustrations © Charlie Brandon-King, 2019. Copyright in the Work © GMC Publications Ltd, 2019. ISBN 978 1 78708 017 1.
Distributed by Publishers Group West in the United States. All rights reserved. The right of Colin Stuart to be identified as the author of this work has been asserted in accordance with the Copyright, Designs, and Patents Act 1988, sections 77 and 78. No part of this publication may be reproduced, stored in a retrieval system, or transmitted in any form or by any means without the prior permission of the publisher and copyright owner. While every effort has been made to obtain permission from the copyright holders for all material used in this book, the publishers will be pleased to hear from anyone who has not been appropriately acknowledged and to make the correction in future reprints. The publishers and author can accept no legal responsibility for any consequences arising from the application of information, advice, or instructions given in this publication. A catalog record for this book is available from the British Library. Publisher: Jonathan Bailey. Production: Jim Bulley and Jo Pallett. Commissioning and Senior Project Editor: Dominique Page. Editor: Sara Harper. Managing Art Editor: Gilda Pacitti. Color origination by GMC Reprographics. Printed and bound in China.